**Tomorrow
is a Matter
of Choice**

**Tomorrow
is a Matter
of Choice**

Tomorrow
is a Matter of
Choice

An 8-Step Action
Plan for Today

WILLIAM L. THRASHER JR.

MOODY PUBLISHERS
CHICAGO

All Scripture quotations, unless otherwise indicated, are taken from the *Holy Bible, New International Version*®. NIV®. Copyright © 1973, 1978, 1984 by International Bible Society. Used by permission of Zondervan Publishing House. All rights reserved.

Scripture quotations marked NASB are taken from the *New American Standard Bible*®, © Copyright The Lockman Foundation 1960, 1962, 1963, 1968, 1971, 1972, 1973, 1975, 1977, 1995. Used by permission.

Scripture quotations marked NLT are taken from the *Holy Bible, New Living Translation*, copyright © 1996. Used by permission of Tyndale House Publishers, Inc., Wheaton, Illinois 60189. All rights reserved.

Scripture quotations marked AMP are taken from the *Amplified Bible, Old Testament*, copyright © 1965, 1987 by The Zondervan Corporation. *The Amplified Bible, New Testament*, copyright © 1954, 1958, 1987 by The Lockman Foundation. Used by permission.

Library of Congress Cataloging-in-Publication Data

Thrasher, William L.
   Tomorrow is a Matter of Choice: An 8-Step Action Plan for Today/
   William L. Thrasher, Jr.
   p. cm.
      ISBN: 0-8024-5400-3
      1. Christian life. I. Title
BV4501.3.T495 2002
248.4—dc21   2002012545

1 3 5 7 9 10 8 6 4 2

Printed in the United States of America

*It is with a thankful heart and deep appreciation
that I dedicate this book to my trusted friend,
business partner and co-laborer*

GREG THORNTON

*who over the course of the past fifteen years, has
been used of God to provide me with a wonderful
example of a person of godly character and
abounding in grace.*

Contents

Part One: Laying the Foundation

Something to Think About   13

The Two Ladders   17

The Foundation   25

Part Two: An Eight-Step Action Plan

Step One: Understanding Who You Are   39

Step Two: Accept Reality   47

Step Three: Establish Your Priorities   55

Step Four: Begin with the Fundamentals   67

Step Five: Practice Good Planning   79

Step Six: Develop Good Habits   85

Step Seven: Stay Focused   97

Step Eight: Keep On Growing   107

Afterword: It's Up to You   113

Acknowledgments   119

Appendix A: What it Means to Have a Right   121
      Relationship With God

Appendix B: A 30-Day Bible Reading Program 125

Appendix C: How to Step Up and   127
      Use a Time-tracking Log

Part One:
Laying the Foundation

Something to Think About

Some time ago in a Sunday morning worship service, I was deeply moved by a comment from the pastor. He suggested that we should take time to reflect that one kind act of giving someone a cool cup of water in the name of Christ will be remembered for all eternity. Fifteen billion years from this moment, all the things done in the name of Jesus Christ will be remembered and celebrated to His glory. In contrast, all the sinful and meaningless acts that have so dominated human nature and the history of mankind will be remembered no more. What we do every day of our lives does have eternal

implications. Our life is cumulative—what we do today will affect tomorrow, and our actions that day will affect the next. Over time we will make a life, but far more important we will mark eternity for good or for bad.

Many believers' lives do not reflect the importance of progressing daily in preparation for that day when they will be ushered into eternity. They have made numerous attempts to live a life that the Bible instructs them to live, but they have not been able to produce a consistent discipline resulting in real spiritual growth and the abundant life they so desire.

Every believer is given an opportunity to live a life that one day could result in hearing the most wonderful words spoken by the Lord Himself, "Well done, My good and faithful servant." It is sad to think that multitudes of believers may miss this experience because they never seemed to be able to pull everything together. They have tried, but their efforts never seem to have any lasting impact.

God's desire is for all believers to reach the abundant life of knowing and enjoying Him and to fulfill His plan and purpose for their lives. God has made available everything that believers will ever need to achieve this goal if they have the desire and obedience to do it.

My goal in writing this book can be summed up in the following points:

1. To reinforce the fundamental truth that every believer has been provided, through the person of the Holy Spirit and the Word of God, everything he will ever need to be transformed into the likeness of Christ.

2. To present a sound biblical approach that will provide a simple method of disciplines that over time can be used by the Holy Spirit to produce the life of holiness that we are called to live.

3. To remind the reader of the importance of today, how our actions of today produce the results of tomorrow, and the urgency to make changes now.

It is extraordinarily easy to waste time,
extraordinarily easy to waste a day,
and ultimately,
extraordinarily easy to waste a life.

Much that pertains to dress,
to accomplishment, to living, to employment,
to amusement, to conversation, will appear,
when we come to die, to have been like the playthings
of children. We shall feel that time has been
wasted and strength exhausted by
that which was foolish and childish.

—JONATHAN EDWARDS

The Two
Ladders

When my wife and I were in college, we learned to play golf on a beautiful "par three" course. The course had eighteen holes, but all the holes were designed for only three shots to go from the tee to the hole. In many ways it was constructed as a scaled-down golf course, with water hazards; some long,straight fairways; and even some with a slight "dogleg" (an angle on the hole from tee to green). One of the reasons we learned there was that it was far less expensive than playing at a real golf course. The course was also much easier to play. Over time we became quite good at playing golf at this level.

A few years later when I had the opportunity and resources, I began to try to play golf again, but this time on a standard full-length course. At this point I became aware of a critical principle that holds true in most areas of life: If you don't master the basics of what you begin to do, eventually you will not be able to reach the standard that is required to achieve real success, nor will you advance in your endeavors.

> **Great things are not done by impulse, but by a series of small things brought together.**
>
> —Vincent van Gogh

I eventually gave up the game of golf because I realized that in order to play the game effectively, I would need to go back to the basics and learn the right way.

One of the reasons I wrote this book is that I am convinced that many people have fallen into a similar trap in the area of managing their lives. Early on, they developed habits or routines that seemed to work. Eventually, however, those habits proved to be ineffective in providing an approach or a framework that leads to growth and satisfaction in the results they are striving for. If they keep doing the same things the same way, they will never have a true sense of what it is to realize a fulfilled purpose for their lives. Their dreams of tomorrow never come to pass because they have failed to properly develop the skills and disciplines required to build those dreams.

A Monumental Question

Learning the basics is vitally important if you are expecting to grow and progress in life, and I will address some valuable steps that will help in this area in later chapters. But there is something far more important than the basic skills, and it is a question that must be answered by every human being. It is the question, "What is my relationship to the true Creator God of the universe and am I sure that I really understand the instructions He has provided in order to have a real relationship with Him?" Failure to understand and correctly answer this question will have an impact on every area of your life as well as your existence in eternity.

When a person has properly understood and dealt with this question, he or she will go back and, in many ways, start over. By the Spirit of God the person has been made a "new creation," and everything in one sense is new. If you are not certain that you have become a new creation in Christ by a supernatural act of God, then you need to deal with that issue first. I would recommend you read my book *Things I've Learned on the Way to Heaven*. It may help you to avoid the mistake I made when I failed to realize my need to ask this question for myself.

A Helpful Symbol

You will note that I have used a simple graphic to illustrate this subject. A person must be a new creation in Christ as the foundation, the solid ground beneath the ladder, or nothing else works. I have chosen to use the symbol of a ladder for a number of reasons. First, it is graphically plain and simple to understand, and you of course recognize that a ladder's purpose is to take you from a lower position to a higher position. A ladder demonstrates upward progression, and a climber needs to start at the first step and move upward one step at a time. Skipping steps can lead to a failure to accomplish the climb.

Another reason I've chosen to use the symbol of a ladder is that it provides a wonderful picture of how the rails of the ladder connect to each step on the ladder. The rungs are formed by being fit into side rails. The rails support and connect the rungs, and they assist in carrying the weight when someone climbs the ladder. It is clear that if you don't have rails to connect the rungs to, then you can't have a ladder.

Everyone is on a ladder. The key question is how good is your ladder, and are you on the right one?

I have come to realize that two "ladders of life" are available to every person. These two ladders have many of the same steps, but the "unifying rails" are

what make the ladders totally different. The first ladder of life I label "the way of man." The unifying rails of this ladder are labeled *self* and *worldly wisdom*. When a person chooses this ladder, the rail labeled *self* is in control and provides the strength and direction for action, and the ladder draws from *worldly wisdom* for its information source and guidelines for operation. The rails of a ladder influence every step. That is why from outside appearances two individuals can seem to be on the same ladder for a time, but eventually these unifying forces will reveal the true person and which ladder of life the person is on.

> **Many men would have arrived at wisdom had they not believed themselves to have arrived there already.**
>
> —SENECA THE YOUNGER

An example of this could be someone who outwardly appears to be a believer, attends church, is a good citizen, works hard and provides for his family, yet something is missing. First, this person does not have the Holy Spirit, so he will never understand the things of God. He will not be able to understand the Bible from a supernatural standpoint. Because he is still dead spiritually, the outward acts are not driven by pure motives but are driven by tradition, social environment, and some sense of the need for religion.

Second, at the core of his being he is driven by a desire to glorify himself—not God. He probably does not even see this himself. No one, in his unregenerate state, grasps the evil motives and selfishness of his own heart. It is only as God opens our eyes that we understand how wicked the human heart became after the Fall.

In contrast, the ladder of life that I call "the way of God" has for its unifying rails (or forces) the *Spirit of God* and the *Word of God*. In this ladder the Spirit of God affects every step that the new believer takes. He provides the direction and energy, primarily through the providential circumstances of life (who we are, how He made us, how we come to know ourselves, etc.) and the Word of God (the Bible).

As we progress on this ladder, we will realize how different it is from the other ladder of life and how transforming this way can be. This ladder encourages us to learn more and more about who God is, how He wants us to learn to enjoy Him, and the wonderful purpose He has for our lives.

Like everyone else, I started out on the ladder of life called "the way of man," but at an early age I thought that I had made a change to "the way of God." Tragically, I was deceived, because my experience was produced by an outward act based on a need to conform, a fear of eternal punishment, and a

poor understanding of what the Bible makes clear is necessary in order for someone to become a new creation in Christ. I was trying to become a Christian by doing something myself in place of crying out to God to work a miracle in me from the inside out, by giving me a new heart. Change can only come from a new heart that only God can give.

Because of this deception I spent twenty-eight more years on the wrong ladder. Like many people, I developed a very effective ladder, which helped me become successful at my career and helped me realize some of the goals I had set for myself at the beginning of my career. The world is full of successful people who have developed outstanding ladders, but, sadly, they are on the wrong ladder. By God's grace at the age of thirty-six, I was led to the ladder of life called the "way of God." I have now spent twenty-two years on it, and the impact has been life changing.

It is my experience on both of these ladders that has prepared me to write this book, and I pray that the message will be helpful, encouraging, and long lasting for you. When you have the right ladder, it becomes a wonderful tool that can be used in every area of life. Even more, it can be used today to help you build for tomorrow.

In a typical week, 41% of American adults attending Christian churches are not born again.
– Barna Research

The Foundation

Early on the evening of July 16, 1999, reports began to surface that the plane carrying John F. Kennedy Jr., his wife, and her sister was missing. As the hours passed, fears mounted that this would play out to be another great tragedy within the already tragedy-torn Kennedy family. Many Americans remembered the somber day when this little boy saluted his father's funeral procession, and then the country watched him mature to manhood over the years.

After days of searching, evidence confirmed the worst. Off the coast of Martha's Vineyard, some of the plane's wreckage was found. An extensive investiga-

tion concluded that the cause was pilot error: disorientation caused by a loss of visual reference to recognizable landmarks. Although the plane was equipped with flight instrumentation, Kennedy was not trained to fly dependent on the instrumentation. No doubt had he known how to use these instruments, he and his companions would have been spared such a terrible ending of their lives.

I believe this event provides an excellent analogy of real life that can aid in driving home the most critical truth needed by believers today. The analogy I want us to think about is the Bible as the "instrument panel" from God that He has given believers to fly the course of life's journey.

Everyone who learns to fly begins in daylight and calm weather. In the early stages of the Christian life, God usually gives us calm weather as we learn the basics of our spiritual development. Soon, however, every believer will learn the necessity of God's "instrument panel" of life—the Bible. If a believer does not begin to learn and apply the truths of the Bible in his own life, he will become very limited in how he fulfills God's desired purpose for his life. Sadly such believers will never be able to learn to soar like eagles or be used in a powerful way by the Lord. They will not only be limited in their potential, but they will be vulnerable to the onset of bad weather and darkness. It is in those periods that God's

instrument panel is most critical in helping a believer avoid what could sometimes be tragic consequences.

God has told us that we will have trials and trouble in this life. Everyone will experience deep valleys and dark times and will need the aid of God's "instrument panel," the Bible. My own life story provides a classic example of how this truth can play out.

When I was a youngster I thought I had received Christ and so I was a Christian. Even though I attended church regularly, I never read the Bible or studied it. I had a surface knowledge of the Bible, but it had minimal influence on how I conducted my life. For twenty-eight years I thought I was in control—I thought my plane was on track. Then, over the course of a few months, my life began to come apart and I began to lose control of my bearings. Somewhat like the flight of John F. Kennedy Jr., haze and darkness were setting in. I became confused and was in grave peril.

By God's grace and mercy I was rescued. I was given a new heart to understand and eyes to see (Acts 28:26–27). Fortunately I owned a number of Bibles, and I immediately went to the Bible. For the first time in my life, I could really understand God's instructions for all of His creatures. In

True Christians are people who acknowledge and live under the Word of God.

—J. I. PACKER

hindsight I learned how off course my life had been. I soon began to recognize just how critically important the Word of God is for believers.

Every believer must begin his life's journey by becoming grounded in the Bible. It is only as this process develops that we will learn the things that are necessary to live out God's will for our lives. Only in the Bible will we learn core doctrines that are necessary to remain on course and continue in faithfulness to God's will. Only through the Bible are we equipped with the safeguard to help us avoid dangerous pitfalls. Most important of all, it is only from the Bible that we learn about God: who He is and what He is really like, what He has done to address the sin problem resulting from the Fall, and what He has provided for us to be reclaimed to what we were intended to be.

Without the Bible, believers will experience very little growth in spiritual development and will ultimately live sad and unfulfilled lives. They will never realize their true calling. They will not sense God's pleasure in their work or service, and, most tragic of all, they will have failed at becoming instruments that God could have used to see others come to saving faith in Him.

Nothing else really works in a believer's life if he is not getting serious with reading, studying, and applying the Bible to life. It is one of the two main

components of the ladder of life that God has provided for us to climb out of the lowlands to higher ground. It is only as we learn to use this ladder of life that we will be able to understand and live out God's plan for our lives.

Several years ago I saw a televised interview with Dr. Billy Graham and David Frost. I have never forgotten one of the questions that Mr. Frost posed to Dr. Graham. He asked, "As you look back over your wonderful career and ministry, what is the one thing you most regret?" Without even a moment of hesitation, Dr. Graham responded with "I wish I had studied more." Think about that! Here is someone who no doubt had spent countless hours in the Bible and in study as he continued to prepare for the opportunities he had to address millions and millions of people around the world. Yet he felt he had not devoted enough time to studying.

Another analogy regarding the importance of the Bible is provided by Scripture itself. The Bible is

> Many Christians remain in bondage to fears and anxieties simply because they do not avail themselves to the Discipline of study. . . . Jesus made it unmistakably clear that the knowledge of truth will set us free.
>
> —RICHARD J. FOSTER

called "a lamp unto our feet and a light unto our path." It is also referred to as giving understanding to our minds. It is important to realize that the light of the Bible extends far beyond providing illumination into the darkness. The Bible does provide light as we travel along the path of life, and it helps us avoid the dangerous pitfalls that are part of that path. But it also provides a light to our heart (our emotions). It teaches us about the love of God, His tender mercies, and His patience and longsuffering. The Bible exposes our heart condition and lights the way for change. It does the same with the mind. The Bible is full of the wisdom of God. As the Creator, He alone has all the light on truth, and He has given it to His children in the Bible.

In the chapter "The Two Ladders," I said that two unifying rails make up the ladder I have labeled "the way of God." The first rail I have just discussed—the Word of God. Now I want to review some important truths about the second rail, the third person of the Trinity—the Holy Spirit of God.

The Bible reveals to us that the primary role of the person of the Holy Spirit is to glorify Jesus Christ. Christ Himself in the gospel of John said that the Holy Spirit came to bear witness to the truth about Jesus Christ, His ministry, and His ultimate purpose.

In what ways does the Holy Spirit glorify Jesus Christ? There are many ways, but in this chapter I want to concentrate on two key areas.

One of the most important activities that the Holy Spirit carries out that glorifies the Son of God is to draw lost sinners to the message of the gospel and to give them a new heart that prepares them to receive and believe the Word of God. Every born-again believer is an everlasting trophy to our risen Lord and will bear witness to His glory.

The Holy Spirit also glorifies the Lord Jesus Christ by the process of reproducing the character of Christ in the believer. As the Holy Spirit works in the life of every believer, the fruit of the Spirit takes form. As it does, Christ is glorified. In this process of transformation, the Holy Spirit, using the Word of God, begins a work in each believer that helps that believer to have victory over self and sin and to live for Christ and His kingdom.

As the believer is taught by the Holy Spirit, the will of God for his life will take shape, and he will be drawn to fulfill his calling. It is in this calling that the believer brings forth much fruit and glorifies his Lord and Savior. But nothing in this process can be done without the power of the Holy Spirit. It is He who provides the power, the direction, and even the motive and desire to please God. The Holy Spirit is the instrument of grace for the Godhead.

I realize every day how easy it is to not take advantage of the wonderful opportunities God wants us to read and study His Word. If a believer misses this, nothing else will work the way God has desired in that person's life. God's best will be lost because the person will miss instructions and directives that only God can give. The foundation that we must have if we are ever to fulfill God's purpose and plan for our lives is knowing and applying the truths from the Word of God. This point is basic, but failure to grasp it will have lifelong and even eternal consequences. Not only do we learn to live out the life of a disciple, but even more, we begin the journey of knowing God as He has revealed Himself in the Bible. As we learn of Him, we learn how to truly love and serve Him and others.

> No one is born physically into the kingdom of God. Rather, entrance to the kingdom is dependent on the Holy Spirit.
>
> —R. C. Sproul

You can ask yourself some critical questions to prepare to develop a plan to read and study the Bible.

First, as I asked in the previous chapter, are you sure you have a relationship with God through Jesus Christ? You must be born again—you must have experienced a supernatural work of the Holy Spirit that brought you from being spiritually dead to being spiritually

alive. It is at this point that the Holy Spirit comes to live in the person who is a new creation in Christ. Many people are religious but not born again.

Many people own Bibles but have no idea what the contents mean. Some people even read the Bible but are not spiritually able to discern the true meaning. You must have the person of the Holy Spirit living within you, because it is from Him and Him alone that true understanding comes. Without the Holy Spirit our minds and hearts will only experience a book of words—no different from any other book. It is the Holy Spirit who gives us a new life in Christ and equips us to understand and apply truth. Tragically, many people are trying to do something that is impossible.

> **Without the Holy Spirit there would be *no faith* and *no new birth*—in short, *no Christians*.**
>
> —J. I. PACKER

Second, have you prayed and asked God to help you to be sensitive to the drawing toward His Word, and have you prayed that the Holy Spirit will continue to convict you of the importance of developing a daily habit of reading and studying the Bible? In a later chapter I will provide some aids on how to develop good habits.

Unfortunately, the twenty-first-century church has many "followers" of Christ in the sense that I follow the Yankees: We dabble in Christianity.

—GEORGE BARNA

Third, do you really understand the importance of daily Bible reading and why it is so critical to your entire life?

Fourth, do you really have a hunger for God's Word and the instructions and guidance it provides?

If anyone is going to get really serious about making tomorrow different from today or yesterday, it starts here. Ask yourself these questions, and be intentional about establishing the only foundation that will withstand all that life will throw at it. What a difference this will have on every part of your life.

When we are led by the Spirit of God through the truths of the Word of God, our outcome is sure. Did you catch that?—the outcome is sure. We are promised by God's Word that if we truly seek wisdom and truth, He will provide it through the work of the Holy Spirit using the Word of God. We will grow in confidence, in spite of circumstances, that we are living out God's plan for our life and, most important, that we are being faithful and obedient to His will.

How to Make Progress

1. Be sure your faith is real.

2. Pray and ask God to convict you of your neglect of His Word and your unyielded attitude to the Spirit of God.

3. Set a goal to read the Bible daily. Start with a commitment to read for fifteen minutes daily without exception. In time, progress further in the time you commit to Bible reading, and work at it until this becomes a habit.

4. Write down your goal and keep it with you.

5. Don't skip a day—keep it up for thirty days.

The church is foundering in a slough of worldliness and self-indulgence. We need godly men and women committed to the truth that in Christ we inherit spiritual resources sufficient for every need, every problem— everything that pertains to life and godliness.

—JOHN MACARTHUR

Part Two:
An Eight-Step Action Plan

Understanding Who You Are

Of the multitude of gifts received when someone becomes a new creation in Christ, one is the beginning of an understanding of who we are as human beings—that God has reclaimed us to form us into the persons we were originally meant to be before the Fall. He begins to fill a void that was never satisfied before, although we continually tried by varied methods. As our new life in Christ progresses, we come to realize that we were created to have a relationship with our Creator and to enjoy Him. As our knowledge of Him increases, we gain a better understanding that we were made in His image and

> **Our life is not our own property but a possession of God. And it is this divine ownership that makes life a sacred thing.**
>
> —ABRAHAM HESCHEL

that He has given us talents, skills, and abilities that He wants us to use to reflect His glory. By submitting to His plan for our lives, we can aid in building His kingdom. The more we learn to understand ourselves, to come face-to-face with how we were made, the more we can be conformed to becoming like God's own Son, Jesus Christ.

We also learn from the Word of God what the impact was on each of us by the fall of Adam. We learn that every area of our being was affected by sin and that even in regeneration—being made a new creation in Christ—we still possess a part of the old nature called our flesh that will never be cleaned up. We realize how far off the mark mankind has fallen, how far off the mark we were, and we begin to grasp the challenge that a new believer faces. God allows our comprehension of these revelations to be progressive so that we are not completely overcome with fear and despair.

Had God revealed all that would transpire with the children of Israel on their journey to the Promised Land, few would have been willing to leave Egypt. In my own life, if God had revealed what I would need

to go through in order to grow in my new life in Christ, I would have not been able to cope with it. God has taught me a great principle to live by—that life is progressive. We are directed to focus on today and not be so concerned with the fears of tomorrow that we never address what could and should be done today.

> Even if we do not realize the fact now, the most terrible result of sin is that it cuts us off from God.
>
> —JOHN STOTT

We also begin to sense the importance of what comes after this life. Things that in the past consumed our attention and effort seem to be far less important and sometimes almost irrelevant. As we reflect more and more on who God is and why He created us, the priorities of our lives start to change.

Purposing to make our lives count for eternity is one of the manifestations of becoming a new creation in Christ. As true believers we recognize that something has happened that affects the way we think. It may be very slight at first, but in some cases it can be a profound change, somewhat like going from darkness to light. Along with this changed perspective something else happens: We change the way

> You are younger today than you ever will be again. Make use of it for the sake of tomorrow.
>
> —ANONYMOUS

we view ourselves and what we think about ourselves. When a person is born again and converted, one of the things that occurs is that that person experiences a strong compulsion to confront his sins, to turn from them and turn to God for forgiveness. This is one of the initial works of the Holy Spirit. He helps us recognize our sinfulness.

The Bible is clear that without an act of repentance coupled with faith, a person has not experienced true conversion. We recognize that who we thought we were and who we really are are quite different. As a new believer grows in the faith, this process should continue. Like most of the things that take place when we become believers, this process of growing in an understanding of ourselves should be ongoing. We should continue to desire, seek, and pray for the action of the Holy Spirit to bring sins to our attention that we need to recognize and repent of. The instrument that is most often used is the Word of God. Repentance takes place as we read, study, and meditate on God's Word.

The Holy Spirit does use other means to bring an awareness of our sins to the surface. Sound Christian literature is one tool that the Holy Spirit may choose to use. A fellow believer's comments or questions can convict us. Our consciences as new creations also become very sensitive to the prompting of the Holy Spirit. But it is extremely important

to understand that this work of the Holy Spirit is not forced on us. Yes, it is true that we are drawn to cooperate with Him, but at the same time we can develop the habit of resisting His leadings.

I am convinced that one of the great sins of many who claim the name of Christ is that they have not fully submitted to the work of the Holy Spirit. Many believers reach certain levels of spiritual maturity and resist the work of the Holy Spirit to take them further. They are willing to settle for some of the surface work of

> It is an exercise in sanity to trust Him. It is growing sanity to commit all of your life to Him. In the light of His claims and the full revelation of Scripture, any other life is crazy. . . . The supremely sane life is one that is totally committed to Him.
>
> —R. Kent Hughes

ridding themselves of obvious sin, but they resist a deeper search to get at sins of their hearts. Until people are willing to open up the deeper parts of their hidden lives, they will hamper the Spirit of God's work and will have very little impact for Christ and His kingdom.

Not only do believers often avoid dealing with many of the deeper sins of the heart (especially the motives behind things we do or don't do), but we

also don't accept how God made us. It is very easy for all of us to covet how God has made others and to be envious of what they have been given. This discontent causes us to be disappointed with what we lack. We live in a culture and time when man's wisdom has replaced God's wisdom even for many believers. We have allowed the world to so penetrate our thinking that in many ways we behave the same as unbelievers.

> **A whole new generation of Christians has come up believing that it is possible to "accept" Christ without forsaking the world.**
>
> —A. W. TOZER

One example of the way many believers make the same mistake as unbelievers is that we get caught up in the status and success syndrome. We make decisions that are strongly weighted toward the potential of earning and the status associated with a career instead of God's calling for our life.

Another example is that we can fall into the envy trap, in which we become preoccupied with how God is blessing others or how He is using them. We fail to look at how God has made us and don't strive to apply His workmanship in us by doing what He wants us to do. Many believers waste a lot of time and effort in attempting to be something that God did not make them to be.

Most never succeed, and the few who finally reach their goal find that it is not fulfilling.

Here is a simple outline that will help you stay on the right course to becoming what God planned and designed you to be.

How to Understand How God Made You

1. Accept that everyone has limitations, but that everyone has great potential.

2. Learn to understand how God has made you. What are your strengths and weaknesses?

3. Figure out what you really like and where your interests lie.

4. Discover your personality and temperament.

5. Focus your time and attention on those things you are interested in and like, where possible, and examine if you are where God has planned for you to be.

6. Invest time and energy in doing everything you can to learn about the things you like and are interested in.

7. Commit to the long view—everything worthwhile takes time.

STEP

2

Accept Reality

Since the Fall, when sin made its entrance into the world, men and women have been trying to recapture things that were lost as a result of that event, though many of them would never recognize that is what they are doing. An innate sense within each of us communicates that something is wrong, that things are not as they should be. This feeling makes us want to try to

The Fall is an offense to human reason, but once accepted, it makes perfect sense of the human condition.

—BLAISE PASCAL

figure out what it is so we can do something to correct that condition. Many spend a lifetime attempting to create paradise, but in the end it never becomes a reality.

> **We are built for significance. Our problem is not that we search for it, but that we search for it in all the wrong places.**
>
> —Joseph M. Stowell

Some choose a course of rebellion and take out their frustrations in the form of violence or destructive behavior. Others just give up early in life, sensing that there is no hope of remedy. The rest of us are somewhere in the middle, constantly moving toward either extreme, because the realities of this life are hard.

Fortunately for those of us who are believers in Jesus Christ, we have been given the person of the Holy Spirit of God and the Word of God to help us gain an understanding of the world we live in and also a perspective on what is taking place. As we learn the truth about the condition of ourselves and of everyone who makes up the human race, we start to comprehend to some degree the terrible consequences of sin and how it affects everything in life. As we grow in our knowledge of the Word of God, we better understand the real causes of these daily tragedies that play out

around us. We learn that our choices have consequences—for good and for bad. As the Bible makes very clear, we reap what we sow.

Even believers need to grasp some hard truths that are essential if we are going to become what God desires for all of His own. To really understand the problem, we must go back to the book of Genesis in the Bible to better comprehend what God put in place because of the sin of Adam and Eve and the actions of the serpent.

In addressing and confronting the serpent, God put a curse on him above that of every other living thing on this earth. He also initiated global warfare between the forces of the devil and the people of God. It is a monumental but tragic fact that most believers simply have overlooked or have been deceived to think it isn't true.

Stop for a moment and try to imagine that you were living in Europe at the beginning of World War II and you never accepted the fact that a global conflict was taking place right at your doorstep. If you lived in certain countries, you might get by with the denial for a while, but even then you would have begun to notice bad things happening around you. Even worse, you would hear about the atrocities taking place among other people, the stories about horrible battles, and even rumors about the operation of death camps. Eventually you would have

been confronted with the truth that you were involved in a war. Warfare is a horrible thing, and every believer needs to understand that we are all part of it even though we may try to ignore it.

Recognition of global spiritual warfare is not only vital for our overall understanding of what is taking place between the forces of Satan and the forces of God, but it has very practical implications for how believers should be living their daily lives. The knowledge that a great warfare rages around us should cause us to be continually on guard for actions taken by the Enemy. One of Satan's greatest weapons in the area of spiritual warfare is temptation. In many ways temptation is a little like espionage: It operates in deceptive ways so we let our guard down and become victims.

Another strategy used by Satan is to plant impostors within the ranks of believers. I am convinced that within our churches are many who are enemies of the Cross and do not know our Lord. In most cases they are deceived themselves, but they can still be very damaging to a particular church body. The Enemy can also destroy testimonies and ministries. If we are not continually alert, we will become a casualty of the devil.

In warfare it is critical that soldiers be in training and fit for battle. All believers should be soldiers of the Cross. Every believer is needed in this great

battle, and yet the reality is that many have done little to train and prepare for battle. Many are so ill equipped for spiritual warfare, that when our Lord has need of them, they must be passed over for someone who is ready for the conflict.

As in all war, few are called to fight on the front lines, but all are called to make sacrifices. During World War II every American got involved. Even little children did everything they could to support the war effort. The urgent need today of many of those who claim the name of Christ is to wake up to the fact that we are in a great battle. We need to get trained, get prepared, and get into the fight.

The Consequence of the Fall on Men and Women

The greatest proof that when God says something it is absolutely true and He means what He says is displayed in what happened to mankind after the Fall. God told Adam and Eve that the day they ate from the Tree of the Knowledge of Good and Evil they would die. They disobeyed God and they did die—spiritually they died that moment. They lost all of their goodness, and they lost their ability to know God and to fellowship with God. Not only was fellowship lost, but God introduced other punishments for Adam and Eve. For Eve it was now

to have pain in childbirth and to have conflict between her and Adam. This conflict was passed on to all of the offspring who would follow. This is the reason marriage is hard work, and this is why divorce and conflict between men and women are so common.

> Work is not itself a curse; rather, work is something that is itself cursed by sin.
>
> —Ben Patterson

Likewise, God added the punishment that the earth itself was cursed. The paradise God had made was marred by the sin of Adam. Because of this curse on the earth, man, from that point on, would struggle to do what had been pleasurable. Work before the Fall was a wonderful gift God had given to Adam; now everyone who has lived has seen that work usually involves struggle and strain.

These are realities we need to grasp and to accept coming from the all-righteous and perfect God of Creation. We need to understand and accept that everything that is evil, bad, and under the curse is the result of sin. The only hope lies in the person of Jesus Christ.

It is only as we learn to accept and understand the reality of life due to the Fall that, as believers, we can begin to make a difference. If we become obedient to the calling for which we have been created,

we will be used of God to play a role in reversing the consequences of sin. But it will not come easily, nor will it be without some failure. We must accept that we are all still part of a flawed world. Only in heaven will we find a new Paradise.

How to Accept Reality

1. Pray and ask God the Holy Spirit to open your eyes to the tragic reality of life around you.

2. Study the Word of God and understand the results of the Fall on every human being.

3. Accept the fact that every believer has been called to become a participant in a great war between God and Satan.

4. Begin to work on preparing yourself to be ready for God's use in this great battle.

5. Don't buy into the worldly thinking that if we all work together we can produce paradise on earth.

6. Understand that we all contribute to the problem.

3

Establish
Your Priorities

The third step on our ladder involves an exercise that will have significant influence on all of the remaining steps of the ladder. As you will see, all the following steps use these priorities as part of their role or discipline. This is a step where many believers make a mistake, and consequently their lives do not reflect the best of what God would desire for them to become.

In my opinion, making an effort to establish the correct life priorities is one of the most important steps a believer can make in living out the life of

faith. When believers take the time to think and pray through what it is that God would have them become and what it is that He has created them to do, then they can move forward in life with a confidence and peace that will help in climbing this ladder of life. Regretfully, I am convinced this is an area where many believers say one thing but practice another.

> **Christ came to give us a sense of calling in everyday work. This is where the world is changed, and where the kingdom is built.**
>
> —BRUCE LARSON

Understanding the importance of priorities and how we come to form and establish priorities in our lives is one of the most influential exercises we will ever be called on to make. We need to learn how our priorities influence the daily choices we make and how our choices affect the outcomes that follow.

Most mature adults have learned that our choices do have consequences—for good or bad. We know that, in many cases, a few key choices made at key stages of life have lifelong consequences. We are continually bombarded with the need to make choices. These choices range across the entire spectrum of our lives, and if we have not taken time to establish some type of

priority grid, we will soon realize that we are not fully prepared to handle many of the really important choices life throws at us.

It is also important to recognize that when we do not make a choice, in fact we have made a choice. Procrastination and avoidance are choices also, and they too have consequences.

How Do We Establish Life Priorities?

In an attempt to answer this important question, let's refer back to the symbol of a ladder I introduced earlier to depict the way we make progress in our journey of life. I contrasted the two ladders that every human being is climbing. One is the ladder of man, which uses self and worldly wisdom to form the essential rails that hold the steps. The other is the ladder of God, which depends on the person of the Holy Spirit and the Word of God to form the rails that influence and interface with each step we take on that ladder.

Nowhere is this contrast more clearly seen than in how differently believers should approach and establish their life priorities versus how nonbelievers approach this exercise.

How Life Priorities Are Developed by the Nonbeliever

There is one basic way the nonbeliever usually establishes priorities. It is consistent with what social scientists have discovered from numerous studies and analyses that helped them develop what is referred to as the primary pyramid of need of human beings.[1] Based on this approach (and I would interject that I believe this conclusion for the non-believer is clearly valid), the fundamental and most critical need of human beings is to survive. It is a natural and normal instinct for most people to do whatever possible to live. After survival comes the need for security. Actually security is linked to survival in that it addresses fundamental needs, both physically and emotionally—needs that provide us a sense of security and the feeling that we are beyond danger or loss of life.

Following the instincts of survival and security comes the need for love. The need for love is seen at the very beginning of life, and it does not subside all through life. When people experience a lack of love, it can result in the manifestation of serious problems. Many would argue that most relationship problems result from the unfulfilled need to be loved.

Next comes the need to have self-esteem. Self-worth (another label for this need) is in many ways

related to the need for love. If we do not experience proper love we begin to doubt our own worth. Many times we are driven to seek self-esteem in ways that ultimately prove destructive and do not produce self-esteem. This need is so powerful in the natural person that people will go to great lengths to produce an accomplishment or relationship that they think will give them the sense of self-worth.

These first four needs on the pyramid of basic needs of an individual play a critical developmental role in the personality and build a sound emotional foundation in children growing up. If the fear of death and lack of security are present, it will have a permanent impact on that child's personality. The same is true of a lack of love, which will generally lead to a person with low self-esteem.

As the first four basic needs are met, a person begins to have a need for self-expression and self-fulfillment. This need provides people with the drive to succeed and to achieve.

Next is the natural desire to grow intellectually, to build up our knowledge, to learn and explore new areas of interest or new ideas. Something in all of us wants to learn and gain understanding, but this need rarely surfaces if our foundational needs are not met first.

Last comes the need to address something inside each of us that we categorize as spiritual. The history

of mankind demonstrates that we are all drawn to some form of religion in an attempt to meet the spiritual need that is basic to everyone. For the natural person this need, like that of the intellectual need, can become consumed by a preoccupation with more basic needs such as survival, security, love, and self-worth.

This then is how nonbelievers operate regarding the basic needs of life, and this is how they establish their priorities:

1. Survival of self

2. Security of self

3. Love needs of self

4. Self-worth

5. Self-expression

6. Intellectual self-fulfillment

7. Spiritual self-fulfillment

The above priority list reveals an important point that can help a believer understand why nothing a nonbeliever does is ever acceptable to God. The reason is rooted in the fact that it is the motive behind the action that reveals the true basis for the action. Of course, good works won't make us acceptable to God, but our bad works show our unregenerate hearts. Everyone apart from Christ,

even a Christian acting in the flesh, has self as the center of all things. Even good deeds ultimately emanate from the wrong motive. It is only when we are changed at the core of our being that we become able to do good deeds with the correct motive.

How Life Priorities Are Developed by the Believer

When a person becomes a new creation in Christ, many wonderful things take place in the makeup of that person. First, he or she is given a new heart, which becomes spiritually alive by the Word of God, producing the new birth and conversion in that person. As was the case at the Fall, every part of this person is affected. The person's heart, mind, emotions, and will are all quickened to spiritual life.

Another wonderful gift that every new creation in Christ receives is the person of the Holy Spirit. God gives every believer the Helper to guide, direct, encourage, strengthen, and prompt him to grow in the new life he has received as a gift from God. Through the power of the Holy Spirit the believer is given the supernatural ability to comprehend and apply the instructions and commands in the Word of God.

> Man's chief end is to glorify God, and to enjoy Him forever.
>
> —WESTMINSTER CATECHISM

It is from the Bible that we understand that our chief end or purpose in life is not ourselves, but it is to give God the glory that He deserves and that is His alone. As we grow in maturity we will experience a continual shift from being self-absorbed to becoming more and more God-absorbed. As our transformation continues, God replaces self at the center of our being. As God takes over that central role, the importance of others replaces our self-centeredness. Ultimately God is given a controlling influence on our entire life.

When a person maintains God at the center of life, this is referred to as experiencing the abundant life of full surrender to the will of the Father. When our lives reflect the biblical priorities established by God Himself, communicated through the Word of God, our lives will be ordered in a vastly different way than the rest of the world. We will rest in the fact that our very existence is assured by God's watchcare over us. We know that He alone holds the keys to life and to death.

Our security comes from God. He is present with us at all times. We know we are loved by God and by all who are His true disciples. We have our self-worth in knowing that we are made in His image and that He has given us a special place for our life. We know that we are equipped for a purpose, and

we seek to fulfill that purpose for His glory. As we carry out His work for our lives, we are fulfilled.

The more believers become conformed to the image of Christ in themselves, the more they reflect the opposite priorities from those the world is consumed with. Believers strive to do the will of their Father who is in heaven. They love others because they are prompted by the love of God to do so. They are drawn to care for those in need because that represents the character of love and mercy in their God. As they mature in Christ, they experience a peace and a joy that is like nothing that this world has to offer. They are content with who they are, where they are, how they are, and who they are becoming. This is what will happen when our priorities are established and ruled by the Word of God.

When we begin with God the Father, His Son Jesus Christ, and the Holy Spirit as the central and dominant priority of our lives, this will allow us to properly order the rest of our priorities according to His will.

> **Keep Christ pre-eminent in all you do.**
> —D. L. MOODY

As we become obedient to His priorities, clearly spelled out in the Bible, we will come as close to heaven on earth as anyone will ever experience.

It is amazing that as we order our lives according to the Word of God and God's priorities, we gain

what the nonbeliever strives for but never really realizes. Serve God, serve your mate if you are married, serve your children, serve your neighbor, serve your fellow worker, serve your community, serve the needy. As you do this God will bless you, as the Bible says, with "a cup running over."

Understanding how to establish the correct priorities for our lives is critical, but then we must move forward to incorporate them into our daily lives. Read on. This is where we take the next step on the ladder.

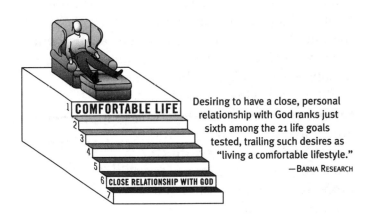

1 COMFORTABLE LIFE
2
3
4
5
6 CLOSE RELATIONSHIP WITH GOD
7

Desiring to have a close, personal relationship with God ranks just sixth among the 21 life goals tested, trailing such desires as "living a comfortable lifestyle."
—BARNA RESEARCH

Note
1. Much of the information for the hierarchy described in this chapter came from David G. Benner, Editor, *Baker Encyclopedia of Psychology* (Grand Rapids: Baker, 1985), "needs," 750–51, and from Phillip C. McGraw, Ph.D., *Self Matters: Creating Your Life from the Inside Out* (New York: Simon & Schuster, 2001).

In a nationwide survey among born-again adults, none of the individuals interviewed said that the single, most important goal in their life was to be a committed follower of Jesus Christ.
—GEORGE BARNA

Life's Goals

COMFORTABLE LIFE
POPULARITY
ENTERTAINMENT
TIME WITH FRIENDS
FUN
PROSPERITY

COMMITTED FOLLOWER OF JESUS

How to Establish Your Priorities

1. Examine the motives that affect your daily decisions.

2. Be intentional about placing God at the center of everything you do.

3. Make the reading and study of God's Word your top priority every day.

4. Establish prayer as a continual action of your life.

5. List these and other priorities of your life, and put them in order.

6. Learn to depend on God and accept His providential care and control in your life.

7. Purpose to use the gifts and opportunities God has given you today.

8. Strive to respond to the prompting of the Holy Spirit.

Begin with the Fundamentals

In the preceding chapter I developed the need to clearly define and lay out your life priorities. For the believer these life priorities are built on the foundation of the Word of God. The twenty-one letters of the New Testament provide detailed instructions on the key areas of life and how they need to be applied.

As we read and study the Word of God, the Holy Spirit impresses upon us how these instructions should be exercised in our daily lives. Once we see how we need to live based on these instructions, then we have to learn how to apply these priorities within

> The best thing we have to offer the world is . . . the fruit of our walk with the Lord — what is borne in us from the time we have spent with him.
>
> — BEN PATTERSON

the limitations of time. Each of us has twenty-four hours in a day, one hundred sixty-eight hours in a week.

There are only so many events and actions that anyone can process or produce within the course of a twenty-four-hour day and that one-hundred-sixty eight-hour week. How we manage or control these events and activities determines how well we will use the time that God has given us.

How to Improve Your Time Management

In order to be successful in using your time wisely, you will need to determine how much time each of your priorities requires and how this will play out in the course of a given day. Since there are usually variations from day to day, you will need to figure out what can be done in each of the seven days that make up a week. An effective use of your time will require that you address the entire week as you plan your schedules for each day of the week.

It is from this process that a person learns how to improve the ability to manage the use of time.

Sometimes we cannot control events or circumstances in our lives. This is part of life, and the only thing we can do on these occasions is accept it and work around those unexpected interruptions.

It is important to be reminded that each day God gives us a fixed number of hours and numerous opportunities to be good stewards. Ordering our lives each day to reflect these responsibilities will change the way we live and the way our tomorrows turn out.

An Important Next Step

As you can see from the steps on the ladder that you have already taken, some organizational tool would be very beneficial to you and would provide a place to write down the priorities, schedules, and plans that you want to address on a daily and weekly basis.

It is reported that the only surviving relic from the youth of John D. Rockefeller is a simple ledger that he had maintained

The laws of unseized time come back to haunt the disorganized person again and again, until he decides to gain the initiative before everyone and every event does it for him.

—GORDON MACDONALD

when he started out on his own. In this ledger he recorded, day by day, his income and expenses, what he set aside for savings, and the amount he purposed to invest. It also contained every contribution he gave to church and to charity—which consistently totaled 10 percent. Most fascinating of all was that every entry of this information was kept down to the precise penny.

This ledger speaks volumes about the man who wrote it and how he became one of the richest men in the world. Early in life John D. Rockefeller learned and practiced a fundamental principle that served him well the remainder of his life. He recognized the value of keeping a written record and how it allowed him to make shrewd decisions and build for the future.

> Where no plan is laid, where the disposal of time is surrendered merely to the chance of incident, chaos will soon reign.
>
> —Victor Hugo

Keeping a Record Will Always Be Beneficial

Not only will keeping a record be beneficial in regard to the specific area that you are tracking, but it will prove to be helpful in a number of other ways, especially for planning and goal setting. One

of the best ways to manage your financial resources is to keep good records in writing so that you are aware of where you stand financially. Keeping tabs on one's money is important, and many people tend to do this fairly well. But interestingly enough, when it comes to time it is surprising how few people keep track of what they have done with the time they have. I believe this is one of the major contributing factors to why so many people struggle with trying to use their time wisely. Very few people really have a clear picture of how most of their time is spent. They make the mistake of thinking about their time only in large segments, such as "Well, I go to work, come home, eat dinner, watch a little TV, read the paper, and get ready for bed."

Most people believe that their days are fairly full, when in reality a sizable portion of their time is wasted. If they applied this foundational principle of keeping a simple record of where they spend their time, they would quickly discover how easy it is to waste time and yet our time is by far the most valuable possession we have been given in this life.

As people keep better track of where their time is invested, they usually discover that their time investment is not consistent with the priorities that they have laid out. What many people say is

No believer is ever beyond the basics.

—JOHN F. MACARTHUR

important is not supported by the time they invest in it. When people spend considerable time on low priority areas, they don't see much success in making progress in things they would like to achieve.

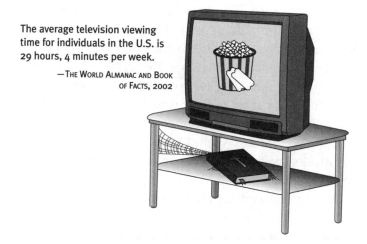

The average television viewing time for individuals in the U.S. is 29 hours, 4 minutes per week.

—THE WORLD ALMANAC AND BOOK OF FACTS, 2002

As I have been in the business world for more than thirty-five years, one of the most important measurements I've learned to observe is called "return on investment." What it means is simply this: Every business needs to measure all the costs associated with doing something (a new product, a new program, a new operation, etc.), and then measure what value or profit, over time, something produces.

What Do You Get from the Investment You Make?

As individuals, especially believers, we also need to understand this concept and apply it to our lives.

Let's look at our lives applying this concept. First, we have our existence, which was given to us by God. Every life is of incalculable worth. Every life is purposed to make a contribution, and each person is given a certain amount of time. This time can be used to produce very valuable results such as investing in someone else's life, helping those less fortunate, or providing various types of goods or services. We are given talents and abilities from God that He intends for us to develop and use. We are given varied opportunities every day that we can choose to take advantage of or waste. All of these are "investments" that God makes in each of our lives.

> Our value is not dependent on our ability to earn the fickle acceptance of people, but rather, its true source is the love and acceptance of God. He created us.
>
> —Robert S. McGee

The key questions that we need to ask ourselves are how are we going to use these investments from God, and what kind of results are we going to expect

from each investment. This is why tomorrow is a choice. We can determine that we are going to work to maximize these investments to the fullest degree, or we can miss many opportunities and miss the chance to employ the contribution and difference we could make. Most believers are familiar with the parable of the talents. One day we will give account for how we have used the investments God has given us.

This reminds me of a saying that I have heard over the years: "A mind is a terrible thing to waste." Sadly, many minds are wasted because people don't think about getting the best return on investment. They don't stop to realize that our lives are a gift of opportunity from God and that we have a responsibility to produce a good return on that investment.

> It is true that the things we are entertaining in our minds today determine what we will be in the future.
>
> —JIM PETERSON

Over the course of my life I have learned some important disciplines that have helped me realize a very good return on investment in my natural as well as my spiritual life. I assure you that, if you apply these fundamentals to your daily life, they will greatly increase your return, and it will amaze you how helpful and beneficial these disciplines will be. Let's look at just a couple of these.

First and foremost, maintain fellowship with God. Pray and ask God to guide and direct your efforts and plans, and read and study His Word for wisdom and guidance. Learn to discern what are your priorities and allocate time to them.

Second, purchase or develop an organizing system that will help you pull together the things you need to allow you to address and respond to the priorities that you have established.

Third, make it a practice to write everything down in this organizing system. Keep your priority list with you. Keep your time invested. Keep a "things to do" list. Keep a calendar. Keep important dates. Keep your written goals. If you are a professional, I am the general editor of a wonderful life management system called the *Believer's Life System.* It was designed to provide a tool that precisely fulfills the things that I am addressing in this book. For those who don't need a full life system, Moody Publishers has another unique product called *Life Essentials.* This is a loose leaf binder that helps a person in his or her spiritual growth. Check out these products on the Moody Publishers Website (www.moody publishers.com).

> You can do more than pray after you have prayed. But you can never do more than pray until you have prayed.
>
> —A. J. Gordon

When you write things down, that immediately makes them more important, and it allows you to go back and review information. When everything is kept in one place, nothing gets misplaced or lost. Lost time to locate things is eliminated. You can put devotionals, prayer journals, portions of Scripture, articles, and sermon notes in the system, and because you keep this system with you when you are traveling, it helps you always have reading material at hand and information that you can review.

How to Begin with the Fundamentals

1. After determining your priorities, order the use of your time in a way that supports those priorities.

2. Recognize the importance of making the most of the time and opportunities God has given you.

3. Examine how you are investing the time God gives you by keeping a detailed record.

4. Examine the type of "return on investment" of your time and opportunity that you are getting for the glory of God.

5. Develop or purchase an organizer that fits your needs to consolidate and focus on your priorities.

6. Learn to write things down in your organizer; always keep it with you, and reference and update it daily.

7. Always keep some portion of the Word of God close at hand so you can use otherwise unproductive time wisely.

5

Practice Good Planning

My first recollection of the importance of planning took place when I was in kindergarten. I recall the significance that was placed on what we should do in the event of a fire. My teacher took time to explain the specifics of the plan, even showing us a drawing of it. The importance of the plan was reinforced by having us regularly practice carrying out the procedures.

From those early days of life I have grown to understand just how important good planning is. I have experienced the payoff that comes from this habit, and I have endured the consequences of

the failure to plan well or not plan at all. Most circumstances of life will be significantly affected by a failure to do good planning.

In my book *Basics for Believers,* volume one, I wrote a brief overview of how to begin good planning. If you have never had the opportunity to practice this discipline, my book could be very helpful.

Why Is Planning So Critical?

First and foremost, planning is part of what God has designed in the way life works. We can see it in the nature God has made. There are seasons to the year: a time to cultivate and plant, a time to wait and work on the growing process, and a time to harvest. For thousands of years farmers have made plans and provisions to work according to the cycles of nature.

We even see planning in God's judgment as we recall the story of Noah and the building of the ark. God laid out specific details on how He wanted Noah to build the ark. God knew the necessary dimensions, how the craft would need to be structured, and even the materials to be used. The Word of God tells us that in faith Noah followed God's plans to the letter and escaped God's wrath on a perishing world.

In the book of Proverbs God has told us that "good planning and hard work lead to prosperity,

but hasty shortcuts lead to poverty" (21:5 NLT). The clear fact is that planning is biblical. The God of the universe has purposed to work by planning. The entire story of the history of time is part of God's great plan that we have yet to fully understand. Fortunately a significant portion of God's master plan has been revealed to us in the coming of His Son, Jesus Christ. The Bible is the revelation of the plan of redemption that God has worked out to save for Himself a group of people that will love Him, serve Him, and spend eternity with Him.

God is sovereign over our exercise of planning. The Bible warns us not to presume on God, and yet it instructs us to order our lives by good planning. This balance can be achieved by maintaining an attitude that our plans are always framed in prayer and submission to the circumstances that God has allowed in our lives. Our plans should reflect the wisdom that God has made available in His Word, and we should continually seek the guidance of the Holy Spirit. When these actions are involved in our plans, we can feel confident of God's blessing on

A certain type of planning is condemned in Scripture: planning that does not recognize our dependence on God for the successful execution of those plans.

—JERRY BRIDGES

them. Our planning should also reflect the realities of who we are, our abilities and limitations, and the circumstances that we are confronted with.

Planning and Hard Work Go Together

Notice what the Word of God has to say regarding planning and hard work. They go together! Planning is vital if we are to accomplish our goals, but planning without implementation and hard work will produce nothing. Good planning must be acted upon, and I will address that in more detail in the next step, developing good habits.

Nothing is more terrible than activity without insight.

—CALVIN COOLIDGE

It is also important to note that hard work without planning will produce far fewer results. In my years in the business world, I have seen this played out over and over, when some individuals would work extremely hard and accomplish far less than those who combined good planning with appropriate hard work. Like so much in life, a balance usually renders the best results.

The Importance of Planning in the Spiritual Areas of Life

Planning is critical in the area of our work and family life. Planning is even important in the physical disciplines of life. But nowhere is planning more important than in the spiritual development of our lives. Without planning and hard work in this area, we will not develop as God has intended, and eventually we will become stunted in our spiritual abilities. That condition will affect every other area of our life.

Failure to implement good planning will be one of the greatest mistakes we make in this life because of the impact our spiritual health has on every other area of our life.

How to Practice Good Planning

If we truly ordered our lives according to the biblical idea of work, we would ask ourselves and our work not "How much will I make?" but "Will this work use my abilities and gifts to the fullest?"

—BEN PATTERSON

1. Pray and ask God to help you understand and commit to planning.

2. Begin by reviewing the priorities list you produced in Step Three.

3. Working with your priorities, determine what may be possible for you to accomplish.

4. As you write out and develop a plan, it will surface possible conflicts.

5. Allow appropriate time for all of your important tasks.

6. Avoid over-planning and the expectation of perfection. Good planning takes practice and patience.

7. Always write out your plans, but keep them simple.

8. Keep your plans with you, and review them often.

Develop Good Habits

An alarming trend that is becoming one of our nation's most serious health problems is the substantial increase of those who are considered to be obese. The most recent statistics reveal that 27 percent of the adult population now falls into this category. Obesity is a very serious condition because it can lead to the development of many other life-threatening medical problems. Sadly, this condition is in most cases caused by developing the bad habits of overeating and of doing little or no exercise. Most bad habits don't happen all at once but come on slowly over time until these practices are just a natural part

of our daily routine. Bad habits become part of our lifestyle, and they are very natural to us. This is one reason that it is so difficult to break a bad habit. When a practice has become part of our daily routine and it makes up a normal part of our day, even when we want to try to avoid doing it, the same routine continually reminds us of what we would like to be doing.

> **Living for God is day by day. Choose it.**
> —JAMES MACDONALD

Another frustrating thing about bad habits is that most of them are easy to develop. One of the realities of life is that it is very easy to do the wrong thing. We don't have to work hard to do things that will over the long run be of little value and in most cases will be destructive to us.

It is because of these realities that it is so important to learn the process of how to develop good habits.

One of the most important steps in developing good habits is to understand and accept that most of us human beings are creatures of habit. Habits are part of our daily routine, and they serve a valuable purpose in how we do things. With many of our daily routines we don't even think about what we are doing; we just carry out the activity and move on. These habits, such as washing our face, brushing our teeth, and combing our hair, are common, repeatable activities that are a part of getting started each morning. This is repeated in how we get

dressed, how we travel to work, and how we get started with our daily work role. So the pattern goes throughout the entire day.

By the end of the day, most people have gone through numerous routine activities. As we see how much of what we do every day is driven by habit, this is when we begin to appreciate how important it is to develop good habits.

One valuable exercise that will drive home this point is to keep a record of everything you do by five-minute segments throughout the next few days. You will be amazed at how many routine things you do over and over. The habits you develop will have a profound impact on your life.

> I long to accomplish a great and noble task, but it is my chief duty to accomplish small tasks as if they were great and noble.
>
> —HELEN KELLER

The next step is to take time to review your life priorities. Be sure you have thought through and written out what those priorities are, and ask yourself if what you do every day reflects these priorities.

A Word of Caution

One of the greatest mistakes a person can make is to fool himself by saying one thing and yet doing

something quite different. Many people say that God is the most important thing in their life, but their daily habits say something far different.

As I said in Step 3, the vast majority of people are driven by self as the primary priority in life, and the motives associated with satisfying self form the habits of these people. This is why Christ confronted the Pharisees of the New Testament with the piercing question about motive. They were very religious, but it was the motive behind the action that Christ saw. Be sure that you understand your motives. You must have a heart that is predisposed to want to do the things that are called for by the Word of God and prompted by the Spirit of God.

One out of 3 born-again individuals is [still] trying to ascertain the meaning and purpose of their life.

—Statistic from George Barna's Boiling Point: It Only Takes One Degree—Monitoring Cultural Shifts in the 21st Century

A Proven Plan

As a believer you have become a new creation in Jesus Christ and you have been given the third person of the holy Trinity to come and live within you. Because Christ Himself now lives within you through the Holy Spirit, you have at your core a new motive, and that motive is the desire to please your heavenly Father (as Christ did perfectly) and keep His commandments.

At the same time three obstacles will continue to present you with a challenge. First, there is the world and its allurements and distractions. Sadly this is where many believers are defeated and never able to really have victory over worldliness. Next is the devil, who continues to resist everything of God, especially those who belong to God. Last is the flesh—that unredeemed part of every believer that still is part of the old nature. It is where the bad in us comes from. It is one of the reasons we are capable of developing bad habits. It is why all of us still fail and sin and why we have to work hard to keep this part of us in check.

Once we understand ourselves and what had been done to make us new creations, we are ready to begin the process of developing good habits. As I have gone through this process I have used a simple, biblical reminder that has helped me greatly over the years.

The Seven Calls of Christ

The label I developed for this simple approach is *The Seven Calls of Christ.* This tool helps us be reminded every day of how to accomplish the number one priority for all believers—to glorify God in everything we do and in everything we are. It provides seven simple action steps that will help us be intentional about putting first things first. It provides a mental checklist that helps remind us of what should be most important every day of our lives.

1. **SEEK His kingdom.** "But seek (aim at and strive after) first of all His kingdom and His righteousness (His way of doing and being right), and then all these things taken together will be given you besides." (Matthew 6:33 AMP)

2. **THINK on the right things.** "Fix your thoughts on what is true and honorable and right. Think about things that are pure and lovely and admirable. Think about things that are excellent and worthy of praise." (Philippians 4:8 NLT)

3. **WALK worthy of the Lord.** "That you may walk (live and conduct yourselves) in a manner worthy of the Lord, fully pleasing to Him and desiring to please Him in all things, bearing fruit in every good work and steadily growing and increasing in and by the knowledge of God

[with fuller, deeper, and clearer insight, acquaintance, and recognition]." (Colossians 1:10 AMP, brackets in original)

4. **LEAD a consistent and victorious life.** "I have set the LORD always before me. Because he is at my right hand, I will not be shaken."(Psalm 16:8)

5. **LIVE a holy life.** "But just as he who called you is holy, so be holy in all you do." (1 Peter 1:15)

6. **FOLLOW and serve Christ.** "Not that I have already obtained all this, or have already been made perfect, but I press on to take hold of that for which Christ Jesus took hold of me." (Philippians 3:12)

7. **KEEP your eyes on Jesus.** "Fixing our eyes on Jesus, the author and perfecter of faith, who for the joy set before Him endured the cross, despising the shame, and has sat down at the right hand of the throne of God." (Hebrews 12:2 NASB)

I have found that this simple approach has helped me break old habits and replace them with better habits. One area where this approach has worked is in my daily devotional life. After coming to accept Christ as my Lord and Savior, I immediately developed an insatiable appetite for the Word of God. I spent hours reading and studying. At the same time, though, I struggled to be consistent in the way that I

spent time with my Lord. Some days I would start the day with an exceptional devotional time with the Lord, but then I would fail to do this consistently.

> **Get into the habit of dealing with God about everything. Unless in the first waking moment of the day you learn to fling the door wide back and let God in, you will work on a wrong level all day.**
>
> —OSWALD CHAMBERS

Then I began to notice an interesting pattern that helped me discover a truth about habits that was affecting my desire to be consistent in keeping God as my number one priority. What I discovered was that generally on Saturday morning I was enjoying an outstanding time of devotion with the Word of God, a time of prayer, and reading and study. But Sunday my quality time with the Lord became less, and then once the work week started, I ended up trying to force the same thing each morning, usually with poor results. What I finally came to realize was that a good habit was robbing me of a better habit.

For years I had been in business and had developed the habit of hitting the day with intense focus and concentration. I had become so consistent with this approach that I did not realize what an ingrained habit it had become, especially from

Monday through Friday. Once I began to understand what was happening, I developed an organizer that, the moment I opened it, reminded me of what should be my number one priority—God! Not me, my work, my problems, my opportunities, my ego, or anything else. Over time I made a list of seven Bible verses or groups of verses that helped me stay focused (which are listed on pages 90–91).

This helped me change my habits so that today, even though I am still involved in an active, stress-filled responsibility at work, my first action every day is to spend time with my Lord. It is now a habit. If I am forced to skip it (which is very rare), I don't feel right. I don't feel adequately prepared for the day, and the truth is I am not. More and more I see the value of this good habit of spending my best time every day with my Lord and allowing Him through the Holy Spirit and the Word to guide and direct my life.

How to Develop Good Habits

1. Pray and ask God to help you develop a list of your bad habits.

2. Take the time to see how you spend your time. Keep a detailed record of each day for a week. (See Appendix B for help with this.)

3. Review your life priorities, and contrast the way you spend your day against your life priorities.

4. Set a goal to give God the very best of every day.

5. Develop or buy a system that helps you keep your priorities in front of you every day.

6. Memorize the Seven Calls of Christ.

7. Remember to do something for thirty days straight—then it will become a habit.

We are in danger of forgetting
that we cannot do what God does,
and that God will not do what we can do.
We cannot sanctify ourselves, God does that;
but God will not give us good habits,
He will not give us character,
He will not make us walk aright.
— OSWALD CHAMBERS

ENTERTAINMENT   **SPIRITUAL**

Born-again Christians spend seven times as much time on entertainment as they do on spiritual activities. — BARNA RESEARCH

Stay
Focused

The date September 11, 2001, will forever be recalled as one of the great tragedies of history. Millions did not just hear about it, but they personally witnessed it, either at the scenes of destruction or by way of television. Technology has made it possible to capture events as they play out, and the video footage of this horrible event is astounding.

We have learned numerous things that we can take away from this great tragedy, but I would like to address one profound truth that I believe may help people grasp the power of focus.

Soon after the events of 9/11 took place, investigations began to unravel facts about what actually happened, the details of how the events occurred, and who was responsible. Within days after the tragedy it was revealed that just a small group of terrorists was responsible for the events that destroyed two of the largest office buildings in the world, produced significant damage to a portion of the Pentagon, crashed three planes in the wreckage of these buildings, and brought down another large aircraft in Pennsylvania—the sum of which resulted in the deaths of nearly three thousand innocent victims. As the story continued to unfold, it was amazing how simple the overall plan had been and how easy it was to execute.

Like most occasions of great significance in history, debate and disagreement will surround what happened on that terrible day, but even within that debate I believe most would agree that this event provides a classic example of what can be accomplished when someone dedicates himself toward a goal and focuses his energies and efforts toward achieving that goal.

In my own life experience I have seen how focus played a critical role in aiding me in my career in the business world. At the age of twenty-three, just one year after graduation from college, I was fortunate to join one of the leading medical firms in the world.

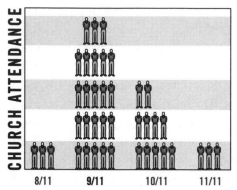

CHURCH ATTENDANCE

| 8/11 | 9/11 | 10/11 | 11/11 |

After the 9-11 attacks, U.S. religious activity surged, but within two months, virtually every spiritual indicator available suggested that things were back to pre-attack levels.

—STATISTIC FROM GEORGE BARNA'S "THE YEAR'S MOST INTRIGUING FINDINGS, FROM BARNA RESEARCH STUDIES"

Through the next twelve years I experienced the payoff of being focused, working very hard, and continuing to grow and learn. Over the course of the twelve years that I spent with the company, I was promoted on ten different occasions.

> **What matters most is what you do day by day over the long haul.**
>
> —JOHN C. MAXWELL

The ascent of the climb was based on the proper foundation of focus, but, sadly, my priorities were wrong. Like so many who attain success in life, I was on the wrong ladder. Thankfully, God stepped into my life twenty-two years ago and placed me on the right ladder. He also corrected my focus from primarily myself to Him and His Son, Jesus Christ. Since then He has taught me that the secret to life is to stay focused on Him and His Word, and then

the other priorities of life will become properly balanced and successful.

Discipline is practiced obedience.

—AUTHOR UNKNOWN

Even today, I can see the great value of focus, especially when it comes to living a life as a disciple of Jesus Christ. I must concentrate on what is most important, not on everything that could be done. Focus has helped me stay on a course of growth in my daily walk with the Holy Spirit and to develop a consuming passion for the study of the Word of God.

Going to the Word of God we can see a wonderful example of the power of focus that took place in the ministry of the apostle Paul. God taught him to keep focused on the goal of taking the good news of the gospel to the Gentiles. If you are at all familiar with the New Testament, you know the reader soon learns of the apostle Paul and what this man endured to fulfill his calling from God. Against continued opposition, physical beatings, and violence at every turn, Paul pressed on to tell many about the gospel of Christ. Even as Paul approached old age and martyrdom, he never hesitated to push on. He never entertained the thought of slowing down or giving up. Paul was committed to finishing the race of life God had called him to. Paul was focused on one

thing—God's grace that has been made available to lost sinners through Jesus Christ.

What Was It That Helped Paul Stay Focused?

I believe we can learn a lot from the life of Saul of Tarsus, who became the great apostle Paul. He was used mightily of God in providing the written foundation of the faith in many of the books of the New Testament and was the person God chose to bring the gospel to the pagan Gentiles.

First, we need to look at Saul's background, his early life, and circumstances that God ordered. Saul was born a Roman citizen. Roman citizenship carried weight and special privileges. He was born in a very religious home of the Jewish faith and was schooled at the feet of the best teachers and rabbis. He became devoted to his faith early in life.

Saul grew up and became a leader in his synagogue as a Pharisee. And finally he became a consumed zealot to rid his faith of the movement called "The Way"—those who followed the teachings of this "blasphemous" Jesus. This was the background and setting for one of the great events in history. On his way to Damascus with the purpose to arrest and bring to trial these rebels, Saul of Tarsus was struck down and confronted by the Lord Jesus.

During this encounter Saul was born again and made a new creation in Christ. Everything changed. From that moment, from that hour, Saul became Paul. He was now headed in a totally new direction. He was now under new authority and with new purpose.

The next thing we see happening in Paul's life is that (after being temporarily blinded) he was led to a stranger's home. Here he was given help and direction. God always uses His children to care for those He has just brought into His kingdom. God has purposed to use people. He could have handled this alone, but He chose to use a man named Ananias. We have all had Ananiases in our early life of faith. Mary and I continue to thank God for Bob and Betts Parschauer who tenderly ministered in our early days of spiritual new birth.

Early in Paul's new life we see the Lord leading him to a place of solitude. If anyone is to remain focused on the priorities that he has established, he will need to get alone with God. In fact, it is essential to get alone with God for a few days of focused time every few years.

The Bible does not provide any details of Paul's time alone in the desert, but I believe that the Holy Spirit taught and ministered to Paul. He was shown the truth about Christ from the ancient writings of the Jewish faith. God had Paul lay the foundation in preparation for his ministry to come.

Paul remained focused because he had allowed God the Holy Spirit to help him build a firm foundation of biblical truth. In addition to being taught the eternal truth of God's plan of redemption through Jesus Christ, Paul also no doubt learned the disci-

> It is impossible to conduct your life as a disciple without definite times of secret prayer.
>
> —OSWALD CHAMBERS

plines of obedience and submission. God will not use someone who has not comprehended the need to submit and obey the commands of the Lord.

Another important element that helped Paul stay so focused on the mission that God had set before him was that he became a man of continuous prayer. Prayer was the instrument that Paul used to set his course, to seek encouragement, and to ask for the energy and strength to carry on. Paul learned early that without the help of the Holy Spirit he would fail in his mission.

That is still true today. God has set forth that if we are to realize success in any area of our lives, it will only come as a result of a partnership with the Holy Spirit. Oh yes, outward success can take place without the Holy Spirit, but in time those things will fail. We can all look back and see when the Holy Spirit was involved in some ministries and when He

was not involved. We need to stay in constant connection with the Lord.

Superficiality is the curse of our age. The doctrine of instant satisfaction is a primary spiritual problem.

—RICHARD J. FOSTER

Last, Paul never got over that day on the Damascus road. Paul never forgot about the amazing grace that saved a sinner like him. He knew it was all of God and that he deserved only hell. Paul continued to be thankful. Sadly, in this day and age many believers have forgotten what we all deserve. They have gotten caught up with their own agendas and their own needs and have lost focus on what is their main purpose in life—to glorify and enjoy God.

Staying focused is extremely hard to do. In our society there is so much to do, so much opportunity. Much of it is good, but in many cases our opportunities rob us of the best. If believers fail to learn how to stay focused on God and keep Him at the center of everything they do, they will never experience what was God's best for their life.

How to Stay Focused

1. Be sure of your relationship with God.

2. Ask God the Holy Spirit to direct you.

3. Get alone with the Holy Spirit and the Word of God and allow them to speak to you.

4. Make use of appropriate tools that God has made available to help you.

5. Continue to pray and seek God's help.

6. Continually remind yourself why you are so thankful to God.

7. Continually review your written priorities.

Keep On Growing

Some years ago I heard what has become one of my favorite definitions of the word *stupidity:* "doing the same thing over and over and continually expecting a different result." It is not a lack of intelligence that produces this stupidity (God has provided an abundance of brain cells even for those who have some handicap), but rather the common tendency to become complacent, set in our ways, and just plain lazy.

Today's society is rampant with those who have reached a place where they are doing very little that is different from what they did yesterday. They are not working to reach that next level or striving to

move into new avenues of opportunity. They just slowly develop a "rut" and then stay there.

I am still learning.
— MICHELANGELO'S MOTTO

The concept of growth is something that every believer should be working to learn and apply both in the natural life and, more important, in the spiritual life. It should be a subject that we continually make a part of all of the priority areas that we have established for our lives.

If we don't grow, we actually go backward. Let me explain. In the arena of natural life, when we don't grow that means we stay the way we are—we keep doing things the same way, using the same approach, thinking we will get the same results we got yesterday. But that approach overlooks a critical fact of reality: Things change, circumstances change, needs and expectations change, jobs and people change—everything is continually changing.

Because things change we must continually grow just to keep up and stay abreast of all that is happening around us. To keep up with all this change requires a continuous commitment to growth.

This is also true in the spiritual realm, but for somewhat different reasons. As believers we know that God never changes, His Word never changes, and His requirements of us never change. But God has ordered a rule for our lives that it is imperative that we understand: If we do not use the light and

understanding we have been given by God the Holy Spirit, we will lose it. If we are not maturing in the things God has given us, we will be losing what we previously received. God does not allow us to accumulate truth that was meant to transform us and just sit on it. We either use it or lose it. God has purposed that our growth should be progressive, and if we stop growing we will experience a regression or backward movement in our spiritual health.

Let me provide one classic example to demonstrate what I am saying. In the early portion of this book I emphasized the importance of reading, studying, memorizing, and meditating on the Word of God. If we are to know God and enjoy Him, we must do those activities. Now here is the point. When you begin the life of a believer, you are not in the habit of reading and studying the Word of God. As you grow, you should experience a growing desire to read and understand God's Word. Over time, if you are growing, you will become more involved with a consistent daily reading of God's Word. You will begin to seek out tools that will help you understand the Bible better. Slowly you

> **The goal is to get the Word into your heart and life and to cultivate an intimate relationship with Jesus, the living Word of God.**
>
> —NANCY LEIGH DEMOSS

will realize just how important this exercise is to everything else in your life. Slowly you will come to recognize that this is the very Word of God, that it is truth, and that it provides all the guidelines necessary to live a life pleasing to God.

On the other hand, if you as a new believer begin to grow but don't develop a habit of reading and studying the Word of God, gradually you will lose an interest in reading it. As time goes along, you will sense a feeling of distance between you and God. Gradually, the world will gain more and more influence over your thoughts, and eventually you will lose the opportunity to be used of God for the purpose that He had planned for you.

> **The less I pray, the harder it gets; the more I pray, the better it goes.**
>
> —MARTIN LUTHER

I am convinced that is where many in the church are today. They have stopped growing and have slowly digressed to a position where there is very little difference in their lives from nonbelievers.

How to Keep Growing

1. Pray and ask God to help you repent of your wrong attitudes that lead to not growing.

2. Ask the Holy Spirit to help you to grow.

3. Understand and address where you are weak.

4. Establish priorities and stick to them.

5. Get organized with a system to help you.

6. Plan some simple steps that will help you grow.

7. Keep it up for thirty days to make it a habit.

8. Stay focused. Don't let other things distract.

9. Chart your progress.

10. Keep the goal in mind.

90 million men are not involved in any kind of Christian growth. That's 11 out of every 12 men.
—Patrick Morley

Afterword:
It's Up to You

As I am writing this book, having lived for fifty-eight years, I realize, like so many before me, how quickly life goes by. Fortunately, I do not spend a lot of time preoccupied with my age or with the fact that I am growing older. What I have begun to think about, though, is the fact that I am now into, or will soon be into, the final quarter of my natural life. Having had the opportunity to be involved with sports, I understand the importance of the "fourth quarter," and I appreciate the urgency to maintain momentum, stay focused on the goal, and finish well.

History is full of those who were on top of life, winning and doing great, only to lose it in that final quarter of life. The apostle Paul talks about running the race of life, and he encourages believers to run to win. Many would ask for an answer to the question, What did Paul mean by the term "to win" when he was addressing to the believers in Philippians 3:14? Is Paul saying that "to win" is to accumulate wealth, to gain status, to produce something that will bring fame and recognition? No! That is the world's idea of winning.

What Paul is teaching these early Christian believers from Philippi is that success, winning, comes by discipline and self-control and keeping our eyes on the finish line. He uses the analogy of an athlete, a runner, to make clear what he is saying. These runners had to train hard, they had to give up things that were not the best for them, and they had to keep in mind the prize or the goal. He was also explaining that, unlike the races that took place there in Greece, where there would be only one winner, all believers have the opportunity to win.

He was teaching that believers win the race of life when they fulfill the purpose that God has for their lives. They win the race of life when they are faithful to God's Word and faithful to keep Christ's commandments. They win the race when they are involved with playing an active role in seeing others come to

true saving faith and grow in their walk with the Lord. They win the race of life when they continue to grow in the grace of the Lord Jesus Christ, when they learn to walk and live each day in the power of God, when they make every decision under the control of the Holy Spirit of God and by the truth of the Word of God. They win the race of life when they keep on growing, even in the midst of hardship, setbacks, and failures. They learn that God uses these circumstances to help believers mature in their faith.

One of the grave consequences of not becoming all that God intends for us to be is that we forfeit the eternal, imperishable reward that the Bible calls a "crown of righteousness," which the Lord Himself will bestow. This prize will last forever—fifteen billion years from that moment it will still be celebrated. It is easy for us to forget this profound truth and to settle for far less than God desires for us. But if we do that, it will be a tragic error that has eternal implications.

> **One life wholly devoted to God is of more value to God than one hundred lives simply awakened by His Spirit.**
>
> —OSWALD CHAMBERS

Let me review and summarize what I believe the Bible tells us about how we should live our lives as disciples of Jesus Christ.

First, we should pause right where we are and reflect on the eternal implications of how we are living our lives day by day. Every day makes an impact on our eternity. Every good deed done for Christ will last forever.

Next, we must understand that this reflecting on eternity can only be done realistically by someone who is truly a new creation in Christ. It is only the influence of the Holy Spirit that will provide each of us with the capability to think in a heavenly way and to accept the truth of the Word of God that reminds us that our good deeds are visible to out-siders (1 Peter 2:12).

We must realize that the life of a believer, if that believer is to grow and prosper, should be directed and empowered by the person of the Holy Spirit using the Word of God as the primary instrument to equip, convict, guide, and sustain that believer in realizing God's plan and purpose for life. It is the Holy Spirit and the Word of God that must be allowed to play a greater and greater role in every-thing we do and in each step we climb on the ladder of life. Without a continual reliance and dependence on the Holy Spirit using the Word of God to direct our steps, we will begin to operate very much like those who rely on their own ability and the wisdom of the world. We will lack the power of God provid-ed in the person of the Holy Spirit, and we will lack

the wisdom and direction that is available from the Word of God for each step of life we take, for each day of life we live.

The true secret to life for the believer is to grasp the possibilities that are available in the power and purpose of the Holy Spirit and to grow in the wisdom and knowledge of the Word of God.

One Last Thing

Throughout this book I reference the fact that it is today that we need to be concerned about, for what we do today affects tomorrow. There is an important consideration that I want to address as I bring this book to conclusion.

The Bible reminds us that our days are numbered by God. We do not know how many days we have been given by God's sovereign design. Therefore, it is imperative that we do not presume on how many more tomorrows we may have the privilege to live. By God's grace we are given many daily opportunities to respond in obedience and faithfulness to these opportunities and to become what God desires that we might become.

> **The future comes one day at a time.**
>
> —DEAN ACHESON

Every breath we breathe is a gift from God.

—JERRY BRIDGES

Don't delay! Don't wait for another tomorrow. Begin to make a change today. Make today the beginning of a journey that will count for all of eternity. We all get only one opportunity at life.

Remember—tomorrow is a matter of choice. It's up to you.

We can't relive yesterday and mustn't waste today by living in a fantasy tomorrow. Only the actions we take here and now can create tomorrow's real promise. We will not have this day or moment to enjoy again.
—DENIS WAITLEY

Acknowledgments

Every book requires work and involvement from numerous people. As with so much of life, many of these people do not receive the credit they deserve. With that in mind, I would like to thank those who helped make this book a reality.

Everyone at Moody Publishers deserves a thank-you because of the level of dedication and commitment they bring to the publishing industry. I am grateful to Greg Thornton and the publishing team for sharing my vision.

A number of people assisted in the shaping and polishing of this book. I want to thank Greg Thornton

and John Hinkley for their valuable suggestions, and Cheryl Dunlop for her editing work.

I want to especially thank Janis Backing for creating the circumstances that were used by God to guide and lead me to write this book.

Kim Falconer played an important role in the overall impact with her research and selection of the quotes and statistics.

As always, I would like to thank my life partner and best friend, my wife, Mary, for all that she does to support my writing.

I thank God for giving me the inspiration and the message to communicate these thoughts to others.

Appendix A

What it Means to Have a Right Relationship with God

1. Begin by asking God (even if you are not sure God exists) to help you find out the truth about who He really is and how you can have a true relationship with Him.

2. Try to honestly examine your life.
   • Are you in bondage to sin?
   • Are you comfortable with a number of sinful habits?

3. Get a Bible or New Testament (preferably a *New American Standard Bible, New International Version, New Living Translation,* or *English Standard Version*) and begin to read the gospel of John. (See the reading program at the end of this book.)

4. Make sure you have a clear understand of chapter 1 and chapter 3 of the gospel of John. Do you grasp who Jesus really is? Have you been born again? Is your salvation from above?

5. Do you see how religious you can be and still be lost? Nicodemus (John 3:1–21) was profoundly religious, but he was lost and needed to be born again.

6. The gospel of John explains that there is only one way to know God, and that is by His Son, Jesus Christ. No one comes to God the Father but through Him (John 14:6).

7. Do you see that all of salvation is a gift from God—the new birth, faith and repentance, and becoming a new creation? We can do nothing unless God starts the process (John 1:12–13).

8. Have you come to the end of your self-effort? Do you understand that we can do nothing that makes us acceptable to God?

9. Have you come to a time in your life when you know that your only hope is to call upon the mercy of God?

10. Have you heard and responded to the true gospel message of Scripture? The Bible tells us:

    a. Every human being *lost it all* in the fall of Adam and Eve.

b. God purposed before the foundation of the world to save for Himself a people whose names He wrote in the Lamb's Book of Life.

c. God the Son, Jesus Christ, came to earth and took on human flesh in order to die as a substitute for sinners.

d. God the Father raised up His Son, Jesus Christ, to confirm the reception of Christ's work on the cross for those who would believe in Him. Christ did it all.

e. God the Holy Spirit comes to lost sinners and gives them a new heart—a heart that comes alive to spiritual truth.

f. The Word of God connects with that new heart, and that is where and when true conversion takes place.

g. Because it is of God, we get it all. We cannot add anything to gain our salvation. We do need to respond to His work, but even our ability to respond is a gift.

h. Now, are you ready to put ALL your faith in Jesus Christ as your Lord and Savior with all of your mind, emotion, and will?

For more information on this subject, please read *Things I've Learned on the Way to Heaven.*

Appendix B

A 30-Day Bible Reading Program

JOHN

Day One . . . . .Chapter 1:1–28
Day Two .Chapter 1:29–51
Day Three . . . . .Chapter 2
Day Four . . . . .Chapter 3
Day Five .Chapter 4:1–38
Day Six .Chapter 4:39–54
Day Seven . . . . .Chapter 5

Day Eight .Chapter 6:1–29
Day Nine .Chapter 6:30–71
Day Ten . . . . .Chapter 7

Day Eleven .Chapter 8:1–30
Day Twelve . . . . .Chapter 8:31–58
Day Thirteen . . . . .Chapter 9
Day Fourteen .Chapter 10

Day Fifteen . . . . .Chapter 11:1–37
Day Sixteen . . . . .Chapter 11:38–57
Day Seventeen . . . . .Chapter 12
Day Eighteen .Chapter 13
Day Nineteen .Chapter 14
Day Twenty . . . . .Chapter 15
Day Twenty-one . . . . .Chapter 16

Day Twenty-two . . . . .Chapter 17
Day Twenty-three . . . . .Chapter 18
Day Twenty-four . . . . .Chapter 19
Day Twenty-five . . . . .Chapter 20
Day Twenty-six . . . . .Chapter 21

1 JOHN

Day Twenty-seven . . . . .Chapters 1 and 2
Day Twenty-eight . . . . .Chapter 3
Day Twenty-nine . . . . .Chapter 4
Day Thirty . . . . .Chapter 5

Appendix C

How to Step Up and Use a Time-Tracking Log

Step One

Decide how you are going to rate the importance of every activity.

Example: Rate by letter grades.

A: important
B: important, but not urgent
C: average importance
D: marginal and of little value
F: a waste of time

Step Two

Determine the level of detail that you will attempt to measure.

Example: The very best measurement is to record every detail of your activity and be brutally honest in how you evaluate or rate each activity.
Another possibility is to use five-minute increments as a guideline.

Step Three

Choose the time span that you are going to evaluate.

The best example is to do it for an entire week.
A good example is to do it for three straight days.
A minimal example is to measure one complete day.

Step Four

Lay out a time-tracking log that you can use to complete this process. (A reproducible form that you might want to use follows on the next page.)

Time-Tracking Log

Ranking: A   B   C   D   F   Date: _____

Time:	Activity:	Priority Ranking:	Time Used:	Comments:

Time-Tracking Log

Ranking:　A　B　C　D　F　　Date: _____

Time:	Activity:	Priority Ranking:	Time Used:	Comments:

Time-Tracking Log

Ranking: A   B   C   D   F   Date: _____

Time:	Activity:	Priority Ranking:	Time Used:	Comments:

Time-Tracking Log

Ranking: A   B   C   D   F   Date: _____

Time:	Activity:	Priority Ranking:	Time Used:	Comments:

Time-Tracking Log

Ranking: A   B   C   D   F   Date: _____

Time:	Activity:	Priority Ranking:	Time Used:	Comments:

Time-Tracking Log

Ranking: A B C D F   Date: _____

Time:	Activity:	Priority Ranking:	Time Used:	Comments:

Thought-Provoking Reading from William L. Thrasher Jr.

Things I've Learned On The Way To Heaven

- *You may believe in Jesus Christ.*
- *You may attend church.*
- *You may even pray everyday.*

But are you really on your way to heaven? Or are you a counterfeit believer, serving a god of your own making on the broad road to destruction?

This book is about the personal journey of William Thrasher, who like many people today believed he knew God and considered himself a Christian, but was spiritually dead until God dramatically worked in his life.

"This book challenges the man-centered tendencies that are so popular in modern religion. As you read, may it also provoke you to higher thoughts about God and a deeper understanding of the gospel."

From the foreword by **John MacArthur**, Pastor, Grace Community Church, Sun Valley, CA

MOODY
PUBLISHERS

THE NAME YOU CAN TRUST.

www.MoodyPublishers.com

ISBN: 0-8024-3745-1

BASICS FOR BELIEVERS, VOLUME ONE

The believer's life is a journey, from new birth to a new home in heaven. In a clear, concise, understandable and applicable way, William Thrasher details 52 insightful commentaries on crucial doctrines and practical issues of today. Each topic ends with suggested action steps and recommended books for further reading on that particular topic.

ISBN #0-8024-3742-7, Paperback
Also available in a Gift Edition : ISBN: 0-8024-3743-5, Hardcover

BASICS FOR BELIEVERS, VOLUME TWO

William L. Thrasher, Jr. continues the tradition he began with his acclaimed *Basics for Believers*, challenging those new to the Christian life and those who have walked the path for years to learn and apply the basic tenets for the faith. He addresses the topics of what we see, hear, read, think and say (and many more), and helps us learn how these affect who we are.

ISBN: 0-8024-3744-3, Paperback

Put God at the Center of All You Do

Believers Life System

The Believer's Life System is an unprecedented tool designed not just to help you organize, but to prioritize. Not just to set appointments, but to set goals. And most important, to help you focus on God in every area of your life. *The Believer's Life System* helps you see those activities the way He does, as valuable opportunities to draw closer to Him.

The Believer's Life System is flexible and designed to fit your own unique personal and professional needs with a family of specialized products. Each *Believer's Life System* has a host of innovative features from time management and devotional helps, to tips on family life and finance -- all keeping God's Word prominent and before you.

About the Author

WILLIAM L. THRASHER, Jr. (B.S. Business Economics, University of South Carolina) began his career with a Fortune 100 corporation in the medical health industry. His advancement through the corporate ranks culminated in his appointment to CEO of one of the company's leading international divisions.

Several years later William started up his own business which he operated until God called him into business-ministry at Moody Publishers. Today he is Associate Publisher and General Manager and the author of three books: *Things I've Learned on the Way to Heaven*, *Basics for Believers, Volume 1* and *Basics for Believers, Volume 2*.

If you have enjoyed *Tomorrow is a Matter of Choice,* you may be interested in additional training opportunities. William Thrasher is available as a speaker to churches and organizations where he relates his life experiences and spiritual testimony. He also trains groups on how to become more effective in their personal and professional lives through his half-day seminar. For more information, log on to www.moodypublishers.com, e-mail williamthrasher@moody.edu or contact Moody Publishers at 800-600-LIFE (5433).

SINCE 1894, Moody Publishers has been dedicated to equip and motivate people to advance the cause of Christ by publishing evangelical Christian literature and other media for all ages, around the world. As a ministry of the Moody Bible Institute of Chicago, proceeds from the sale of this book help to train the next generation of Christian leaders.

If we may serve you in any way in your spiritual journey toward understanding Christ and the Christian life, please contact us at www.moodypublishers.com.

"All Scripture is God-breathed and is useful for teaching, rebuking, correcting and training in righteousness, so that the man of God may be thoroughly equipped for every good work."

—2 TIMOTHY 3:16, 17

MOODY
PUBLISHERS
THE NAME YOU CAN TRUST®

Tomorrow is a Matter of Choice Team

ACQUIRING EDITOR:
Greg Thornton

RESEARCH EDITOR:
Kim Fulconer

COPY EDITOR:
Cheryl Dunlop

TITLE AND BACK COVER COPY:
Michael Briggs, Briggs Creat!ve

COVER DESIGN:
Smartt Guys

INTERIOR DESIGN & ILLUSTRATIONS:
Kelly Wilson & Colin Pritchard
Paetzold Associates

PRINTING AND BINDING:
Quebecor Printing, Martinsburg Plant

The typeface for the text of this book is
Zapf Elliptical